The Weather
RAIN

Terry Jennings

Chrysalis Education

Distributed in the United States by
Smart Apple Media
2140 Howard Drive West
North Mankato, Minnesota 56003

Library of Congress Control Number: 2003070063

ISBN 1-59389-143-1

Produced by Bender Richardson White, U.K.

Editorial Manager: Joyce Bentley
Project Editors: Lionel Bender and Clare Lewis
Designer: Ben White
Production: Kim Richardson
Picture Researcher: Cathy Stastny
Cover Make-up: Mike Pilley, Radius

Printed in China

10 9 8 7 6 5 4 3 2 1

Words in **bold** can be found in New words on page 31.

Picture credits and copyrights
Corbis Images Inc.: cover (John M. Roberts) and pages 1, 17, 20, 23. Digital Vision Inc.: pages 13, 26.
Ecoscene: pages 10 (Mike Whittle), 15 (Christine Osborne), 19 (Peter Currell), 27 (Pearl Bucknell).
Lionheart Books: page 4. PhotoDisc Inc.: pages 22 (Adalberto Rios Szalay/Sexto Sol), 24 (Joseph
Green/Life File), 28 (Adalberto Rios Szalay/Sexto Sol). Rex Features Ltd.: page 9 (Sipa). Steve
Gorton: pages 2, 5, 6, 8, 11, 12, 18. Terry Jennings: pages 14, 16, 21, 25, 29. Weatherstock: page 5.

Contents

What is rain?

Rain is drops of water from the sky. When big raindrops fall hard, we say it is pouring with rain.

Sometimes the raindrops are small. Then we say it is **drizzling**. Raindrops collect on leaves and form **puddles**.

Rain from clouds

Rain is made when tiny drops of water inside **clouds** join together and get bigger.

Clouds get darker and darker.
When the drops become too
heavy to float, they fall as rain.

Getting wet

Rain can make you wet and uncomfortable. In wet weather, we wear clothes to keep our body dry.

We can also carry umbrellas to stop us getting wet.

Houses and rain

Houses have to keep out the rain. The roof and walls are **waterproof**.

Special pipes, called **gutters** and **drainpipes**, carry the water away from the roof to the **drains**.

Rain fills rivers

Some of the rain that falls on hills and mountains flows down as **streams**.

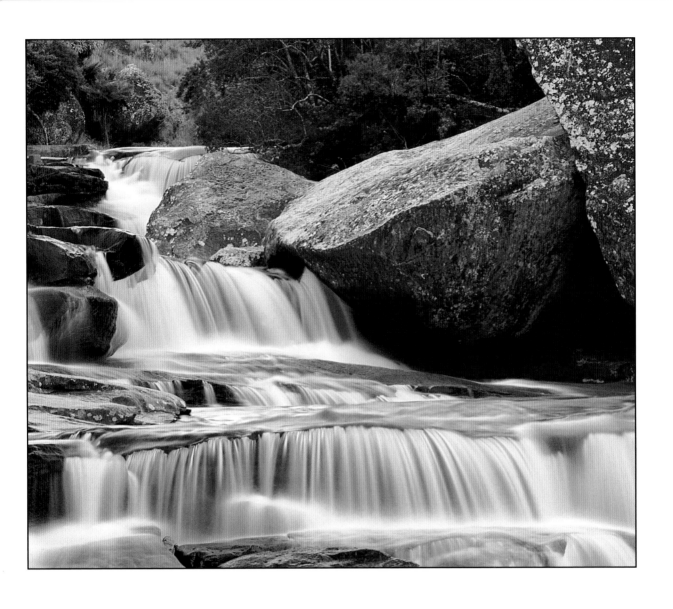

Some streams make small waterfalls. As more rain fills streams, they grow into rivers.

Drinking water

Sometimes a big wall, called a **dam**, is built across a river. This makes a lake from where we get drinking water.

Some people get their drinking water from deep below the ground, at a **well**.

Lakes and ponds

These cows are drinking
from a **lake**. The lake
water came from rain.

These zebras in Africa are drinking from a **pond** called a waterhole. That water, too, came from rain.

Birds and rain

Water birds like rain. They do not get wet because their feathers are covered with oil from their bodies.

Other birds wash in garden birdbaths when it rains.

Rain and plants

All plants need water if they are to grow. The plant roots take water from the soil. That water comes from rain.

These plants are dying
because it has not rained
and the soil is dry.

Rain forests

In some hot countries it rains nearly every day. Huge forests, called rain forests, grow in these places.

Many beautiful plants and animals live in rain forests.

Deserts

Some places have little or no rain. The ground is nearly always very dry. These places are called **deserts**.

Where there is water in deserts, plants like these young **palm trees** grow.

Floods

Sometimes it rains so much that the rivers become too full. Then there is a **flood**.

Floods wash away soil and can damage houses, farms, and cars.

Rainbows

Rainbows are bands of colors in the sky. They are made when the sun shines through raindrops.

The raindrops break up the white sunlight into seven different colors.

Quiz

1 Where does rain come from?

2 What kinds of clothes do we wear when it is raining?

3 What do streams grow into as they fill with rain?

4 What is the name of the big wall that is
built across some rivers?

5 How do plants take water from the soil?

6 What do we call a place where hardly any
rain falls?

7 What happens when rivers get too full of water?

8 How many colors are there in a rainbow?

The answers are all in this book!

New words

cloud a mass of tiny water drops floating in the air.

dam a wall built across a river to hold back the water.

desert a large area of dry land.

drain a pipe or ditch for taking away rain or waste water.

drainpipe a tube for taking away water usually from a roof.

drizzling raining very tiny drops of water.

flood water from a river spreading over dry land.

gutter a channel along the edge of a roof to carry away rainwater.

lake a large area of water with land all around it.

palm tree a kind of tree with very large leaves that grows in hot countries.

pond a small area of water with land all around it.

puddle a pool of water on the ground.

stream a trickle of water flowing downhill; it joins with other streams to finally make a river.

waterproof keeps out water so things or people stay dry.

well a hole in the ground from which water is collected.

Index